THE WILD WILL CALL YOU BACK

poetry & prose by
Gina M. Puorro

First paperback edition November 2021

Book and cover design by Gina M. Puorro

ISBN: 978-0-578-30912-5 (paperback)

Website: www.ginapuorro.com

*To the part of you that has something to say:
may you connect with your wild and free nature,
hear the song of your heart, and give wings to your voice.*

CONTENTS

PART 4: SUMMER

INTRODUCTION

Welcome. Thank you for being here. These pages are an exploration through the seasons of my life over the past three years, born from a desire to express my inner landscapes and how I experience the world around me.

Sometime back in 2010, I attended a workshop and ceremony with an Andean healer. At one point during the ceremony, we all went up to him one at a time to receive a blessing. It was lovely, and after I sat back down, I asked the interpreter what he had said to me. He relayed several simple and short messages, and ended it with: "you will write a book someday." It seemed random and didn't make any sense, but for reasons I didn't understand, I immediately started to cry.

When I started writing a few years ago, I didn't set out to put together a book. I was heartbroken and healing from Lyme disease, and felt like I had completely caved in on myself. Somewhere in the midst of grief, falling apart, introspection, and nursing my body back to health, I was able to finally hear the soft whisper of my own voice that had been yearning to be expressed and heard for so long. I slowly and timidly started to share what was on my mind and heart in a public way, and very quickly felt much less alone in the world. Now, after the gentle and not-so-gentle nudges from my family, friends, and people I have never met, this anthology was put together.

The pieces written here are all a snapshot in time along my personal journey, and I know that words, concepts and my own understanding of the world around me are antiquated as soon as they hit the page. My lived experience is through a limited perspective, and I know what I have shared on these pages will not resonate with everyone, and I am growing and changing with each passing moment. I will always remain a student of the human experience, of the wild and immense force that we have named nature, and to what lies beyond the outer edges of everything we think we know to be true. This book is an offering of love, and my greatest hope is that it will be an invitation for you to share your own voice, and through that, your own medicine.

AUTUMN

...or how to let go

AUTUMNAL EQUINOX

The space
in between
the inhale and exhale
the light and darkness
between planes
of flesh
and spirit.
Gather the abundance
laid down
under the high summer sun
and turn your nectar
into honey wine.
Chop wood
carry water
and shift your gaze
towards the waning golden hour.
Listen as the feathered ones
sing their migration songs
and teach us how to leave
and watch as the four-legged ones
gather their bounty
and teach us how to stay.
The trees are dressed
in their finest
with leaves stained in shades
of fire and ochre
and soon they will show us
the exquisite beauty
of letting go.

Feel the crisp air
breathing on your neck
pulling you inward
and trade sun chasing
for root tending,
movement
for stillness.
Warm your belly with whiskey tales
and mark your fingers with pomegranate.
Put the moon in your eyes
while you scroll constellations across your thigh
and scent your hair
with pine smoke.
Attune your senses
to the sweet lullaby
the bittersweet taste
the rich and fertile scent
of cycles
of seasons
of surrender.

EARTH WOMAN

Your skin smells like fields of lavender
after a soft summer rain
with vetiver and cedar smoke in your hair.
Your voice thunders like wild horses
across the plains
carving canyons into my chest
that echo with my longing for you.
There are ley lines in your palms
ancient stories woven with sinew, blood and bone
tattooing scriptures into my flesh.
Teach me the ways
of cycles and seasons
of life and death
of creation and destruction.
You are an altar in worship and reverence
to the wild.
Supple and ripe
prayers swaying in your hips
nectar and poetry
smeared across your thighs.
I've seen the gods themselves
crack the skies wide open
just to get a little closer to you
and lay offerings at your feet.

LOVE LANGUAGE

Nothing matters, everything matters.
I was born on the outer edges of Autumn
and I feel at home in the liminal space
between what is living and thriving and blooming
and what is dying and sinking back down into fertile ground.
Everything comes undone.
Nothing is left intact.

I'm interested in the gravity that comes
with feeling the impermanence of things.
Of moments
and you and me
and the stories that weave themselves
into the most beautiful tapestries
until one loose thread unravels the whole thing.
Maybe we can weave in a little more honesty to tuck ourselves
into.
I have loved and lost and have been left more whole
with the deep caverns that grief has carved into my heart.

There's been so much talk about unprecedented times
but I think they are illuminating
and I suspect we've been here before.
We've inherited the mess and the gifts left behind for us
and we will be leaving some of our own.
I see your righteousness and I'll raise you
some curiosity and bewilderment.
Any claims to power lose their footing
in the presence of awe.

...

Maybe the next time
and the next
we can bring a little more courage and kindness to our
listening
turn down the concepts and theories
and dial up the context and nuance.

I pray that beauty and art
music and dance
poetry and bare feet on the Earth
will bring us all down to our knees
in reverence to the holiness of wonderment
and help us remember who we are.
Maybe we can all learn to co-regulate with each other
across time and space
with our human and non-human kin
in this vast mycelial network that tethers us to one another.

I want to be a student of the subtle.
Of the soft whispers and sweet hymns
that ride the ocean breeze and the hawk's wing.
A slight pivot towards quietude and the small things.
There are tender spaces
between emptiness and longing
where we just might hear the songs that pass
from ancestral throats to receptive ears.

You contain multitudes—contradictions and stardust and
sacred instruction.
Leave your unanswered question

on the kitchen counter
let them ripen a bit
until their quiet mysteries penetrate you
like bite marks in peach flesh
like a soft kiss at that one spot on your neck.

There's a whole love language
in keeping your palms open while you pray
for when the honey pours down over you.
Sticky, but consistent in its sustenance.

The spirits eat beauty and sweetness.
What will you feed them?

WITNESS

What is it about being witnessed that brings us in so much closer, more at home in ourselves? There's a disruption to the seductive pull of stubborn independence, isolation and separation. A ripening of our fruits. The tenderness of human connection draws us out through the tiny cracks and crevices of our heavy armor, eventually stripping us naked of our defenses, holding up a mirror to reflect our most raw and honest selves.

I have been spending a lot of time lately in circle with others, exploring deeper ways of relating, expressing, and playing in the arena of sacred theater. It has been beautiful, uncomfortable, expansive, terrifying, and joyful. I often ride an arc that moves through pouty resistance and avoidance into ecstatic expansion, with a full buffet of emotions in between. Leaning into the intentional space where I am eye to eye, heart to heart, body to body with others, my whole being can take a deep breath and let go of my tight grip on control, my need for permission slips, and my reflex to hide. I can take in the medicine of witnessing others—letting their bravery, expression, and the sharing of their heart imprint onto my own, inviting me to go deeper, expand wider, surrender more fully.

I recently read about a group of women in Romania who work as wailers: a dying tradition in which they attend the funerals of people they don't know and they cry, wail, and sing songs of mourning. They spoke about how people have lost the ability to mourn publicly, that death has become taboo, crying is seen as weak, and their old ways have been overshadowed by the church. They see their work as imperative because it brings people together, showing those in bereavement that they are not alone, and that their grief is shared across the whole village. They give them permission to feel deeply, and feel deeply for those who are unable to—a way of saying: here, let us show you that nothing you need to express could be too much. What a beautiful offering, and how bizarre that we've been so deeply conditioned to believe that our emotional landscape is weak, excessive, and unwanted, and train ourselves to contain, conform, numb, and push through, even when our inner terrain is on fire.

Your tender being will not be given more than it can handle, but you can only hold so much before it spills over. You are water—the dams behind your eyelids cannot contain the depths of your ocean forever. Let the unraveling be witnessed; it gifts us the permission to feel, to surrender, to release, and to be held through it all with loving hands. Our tears fall with more grace. Our trembling voice carries more bravado. Our words, an anthem of reclamation. The breath that has been sitting in your lungs, trapped under the weight on your chest, can finally slip through your lips with a deep sigh. There is another heart in front of us that says: I see you, I hear you, I feel you. You do not have to hold all of this on your own. Let me share in this love and grief alongside you.

We are storytellers by nature, and a heart cracked-open has more to tell, more to give, more capacity to love. Being witnessed in your anger is liberating; a fire that catalyzes change and burns to the ground what is no longer meant to be left standing. Being witnessed in your pleasure is activating; an invitation to experience the creative, the erotic, the joy that is available to us all. Being witnessed in your grief is expanding; an offering of love and gratitude, an invitation to surrender to the deepest depths of the heart. Sink into the knowing that we all have medicine for each other if we are receptive to receiving, and open to sharing all the parts that we've kept so carefully hidden away from the light of each other's hearts.

WHAT IT IS

There is death and pain and love and beauty everywhere.
I can hear our fingers feverishly dancing
across the cosmic keyboard
writing history and the future all at once
while the here and now carves
primordial symbols into our flesh.
Simultaneously brand new and ancient.
It leaves grit under the nails and spices under the tongue.
I can feel your tears falling down my cheeks
while I sing you a song I don't remember learning
its melody written across my bones.
I see a relative in you—your face looks like my grandmother
or maybe a bear or an oak tree.
It's all the same.
Both the pain and ecstasy sing us to life
the many threads that weave the fabric
of our existence.
Let me metabolize some of this grief with you.
Let me give the depth of my love to you.
I see that inner spark
the flame that dances and flickers
like the sun in your belly
leaving sparkling embers
after it burns everything else away.
Our bodies look godlike
as we dance and pulsate
stretching and expanding
slithering out of old skins.
Shiny and new.

Seasoned and timeless.
Holding many truths at once
and leaving some space in between
for all the questions that may never have
an answer.

LOVE, LIGHT, AND FEAR

Perhaps those who say that fear is the enemy and all we need is love and light ought to try loving with the ferocity and protective nature of wolf or bear or the Dark Mother. Try honoring fear as an old god that has protected us from harm and has been crucial to our survival. Embrace the full spectrum of the human experience with curiosity rather than judgement. Give fear a seat at the table and listen to its teaching without letting it run wild. Find the empathy and compassion to understand that everyone suffers, but we are not all having the same experience.

Perhaps those crippled in fear and panic ought to try taking a few deep belly breaths and ask, where is this fear living in my body? Find the inner child that is trembling and shaking and ask what it needs to feel safe. Try putting bare feet on the earth and breathing fresh air under the warmth of the sun. Welcome in quiet, stillness, rest. Hold space for the grief that ebbs and flows through the body and the thoughts that arise in the mind. Feel gratitude for the preciousness of each moment, for each breath, for each and every blessing.

GROUDLESSNESS

Groundlessness has a dynamic quality to it that can feel exhilarating and freeing, and also thoroughly unsettling (if not terrifying). That liminal space between the inhale and exhale, between balance and falling, between what was and what will be—at the lion's mouth, standing halfway in and half out.

The perceived need to put ground under our feet feeds the desire to maintain a constant state of okayness… to latch onto what feels secure, dependable, reliable. Something to hold onto, something we can control. These reference points give the feeling of having it all together and limiting risks, suspending a false safety net below that will never actually catch us when we fall. No matter how much healing work you have done, no matter how much security you have surrounded yourself with, no matter how much you armor your heart, no matter how much you plan ahead; life will bring you down to your knees, again and again, in the wide open space of uncertainty.

There is deep medicine in this groundless space—free of storylines and conceptual ideas, free of any rules of engagement, nestled somewhere between the question and the answer. Our inherent nature is forever shifting, changing, pulsing, expanding and contracting; it does not walk along linear pathways, but rather dances in an endless spiral, weaving through pleasure and pain, light and dark, death and new life, shifting, evolving, and growing. Trying to resist against these currents requires an exhausting amount of energy that will ultimately result in an addiction to suffering, keeping us feeling fearful, small and separate from the natural cycles and rhythms that teach us how to come together and fall apart over and over.

Can you let yourself continuously unravel, a big beautiful mess, as you let yourself die little deaths again and again? Bowing down, forehead to floor at the feet of uncertainty, offering your fear and confusion in exchange for the exquisite weightlessness of not knowing. Allow your gaze to shift away from scanning the horizon for markers and yellow brick roads, and shift towards the compass of your own heart.

Slow down.

Soften.

Invite grace and gentleness into the fabrics of your being.

Trust that you only need to take the next step that is right in front of you. Let love and grief completely saturate and tenderize you, over and over again. There are countless endings and endless beginnings, and each demand an unclenching of the fists, relaxing of the jaw, deep breaths, and a letting go. Let yourself die, let the old skin shed away, and stretch wide into what is born.

No amount of armor or preparation or planning will change what this excruciatingly beautiful life asks of us—we are not in control and there is no final destination. It can be painful, yes, but can you feel gratitude for the ability to feel your pain-body so deeply? Let your vast expression of love flow through you, fearlessly, vulnerably, and without attachment to whether or not it received. Who knows how long any of us have to live from our own fully embodied expression of who we are, exactly as we are, at any moment. Live the questions —not to find answers, but to sink more deeply into the raw truth and the wild and terrifying openness that comes when you are fully present with what is.

DESCEND

There are things you can only learn
on your knees
or in a storm
or when the cracks in the foundation
of this modern world
open a chasm of uncertainty
beneath your feet.

Your discontent
with what has been named normal
is both grief and longing
for what your mind has forgotten
but your body remembers.

You can feel it
in the way a child's laughter
disrupts your commitment
to what is appropriate
and makes space
for foolishness and magic.

You can feel it
in the way that water
has taught you
how to be a vessel
and how to spill.

Can you trace your lineage
all the way back to salt?

The same that now stains your face
with both sadness and laughter
excites your tongue
and protects your prayers.

You are diasporic. Ecological. Holon.
A vast territory
of many wild bodies
melting into each other
dressed up as human.
Simultaneously living and dying
shaping and dismantling
filling up and boiling over.
Ashes to ashes
stardust to bone.

What language do you grieve in?
What is the mother tongue for that
which twists and contorts your body
wringing oceans from your skin?
The gravity that pulls you
down to your knees
forehead to ground
broken open
at the altar of all you've lost
and how much you've loved.

Can we fall apart together?
Make a commitment

to search for the truth
but promise
to never find it.
Let myths and stories
be the cartograph
for what is both
primordial and brand new
because the present moment
is promiscuous like that.
Compost ourselves down
into the dirt beneath the dirt
and tend the chthonic embers
that light the ancient fires in our bellies.

When the fault lines open
and your mind is grasping
and you don't know
where to go from here;
prostrate
trade rapture for rupture
let yourself spill
and descend.

IN BETWEEN

To the in-between spaces:
May we have the capacity to stay with the tension
of not knowing
May we welcome grief as friend and teacher
and be penetrated by its depths
May we hold the many complexities of human emotions
all at once
May we keep our fingers on the pulse
of the subtlest layers
May we remember that our love was
never, ever wasted
May we move, speak, act, listen, and live
like a prayer
May we learn how to let things die, and die well
including ourselves
May we continue to love with the gentlest ferocity
despite it all

CONSPIRACY THEORY

Where's the nice little infographic
for remembering our own humanity?
How about an easy ten-step guide
to healing intergenerational trauma?
Maybe I'll just start my own conspiracy theory.
I'll make clever memes that will program you
to put down your phone
and go talk to a tree.
I'll share think pieces from secret authors to remind you
that your intuition can't be outsourced
to viral videos and alternative media
anymore than it be outsourced
to politicians or the evening news
and make critical thinking sexy again.
I'll start a rumor that you can trade
your hustle and grind
for some resting and grieving
and watch the whole world take a long overdue nap.
I'll start a movement on how to be
so compassionate and loving
that you will have the audacity to really listen
and care for one another and the land
as kin.
I'll convince you that your confusion and questions
have far more value than the illusion
of certainty and answers
until you finally uncover that
spoiler alert
your great-grandfather was a mountain

who married a thunderstorm
and they gave birth to stars.
You come from a long line
of feathered and four-legged kin
with mushrooms for hands
oak trees for spines
and rivers for veins
that flow all the way back to the First Mother.
She lies just beneath your bare feet
trembling with birth and death
whispering to you
the sacred instructions
that your current form
has long forgotten.
Tell me, what good is your personal sovereignty
and righteous individualism
if you've forgotten the wider web you are woven into?
How slow and sensual can you be
as you undress yourself
from the narratives
of separation?
How badly do you want to get free?

NEVER NOT BROKEN

These are strange and psychedelic times, sitting in this liminal space between what was and what will be; a crossroads within both the micro- and macrocosms. I have been feeling a deep internal shakeup in the way that I always do when met with something much greater than me, bringing lessons of my insignificance and an opportunity to shape-shift. There's been less than glamorous insights into self; meeting places of deep tension between my compassion and intolerance, my flexibility and rigid worldview, my humility and my desire to be right, my longing for and resistance to change, where I remain open and where I shut down... so much friction between what feels like split personalities living in this body. And, in the way that friction does, it's making many little fires in me that need tending, so as not to be snuffed out, or burn me right down to the ground.

I find the demand for a return to normalcy unrealistic and at the same time a frightening prospect. We are writing new stories now—there is never a going back to the way things used to be. We are forever moving, fluid, changing, in a constant state of flux. At the same time, normalcy in the form of the broken systems we have been living in are itching to regain their footing. But our job is not to fix a broken system; it is to turn in towards ourselves and towards each other and dream a new one into being. To summon other powers and worlds and ways into reality.

I am trying to loosen my grip on sense-making and searching for meaning about things that I will never fully understand within the limits of being human. I am trying to approach my beliefs with a light touch. I am resisting my urge to rush towards a sense of certainty. We are human, animal, plant, mineral, bacteria, virus, ancestor, stardust. Where do I end and you begin? With an entire universe in our microbiomes that have the ability to affect our moods and psyche, with every ancestor in our bones, with the complex web that entangles each and every one of us with each other and the worlds around us—who is to say that any thought, idea, feeling or sensation is my own? We are constantly trying to explain what is going on in ways that are human-centric (even when humans are cast as the villain), but who is to say we aren't pawns in a game being played by apples or starfish or bacteria?

I hear the call of many wise teachers and elders singing similar instructions: slow down, get quiet, be still, listen.

What if slowing down and finding stillness has nothing to do with movement or speed and has everything to do with being completely broken and not trying to pick up the pieces too quickly? Rather than striving for a greater capacity to hold more, aiming for total incapacitation and surrender instead. Perhaps it's a good time to venerate Akhilandeshvari, Goddess of Never Not Broken; I hear her asking us to sit with the wreckage and feel the sharp pangs of loss and grief. No expectations of the future, no instructions for how to move forward. A time to hospice ourselves through a good death, and the long slow process of composting our former selves.

What if getting quiet has nothing to do with turning down the volume, and more to do with a subtle attunement towards finding the sacred amidst the noise and chaos, or amidst the mundane of the day to day? A deep awareness and presence with humans, the other-than-human, and the many sensuous occurrences happening all around us.

Perhaps this is the time to call on the trickster—put out some good meat for Coyote, pour libations for Loki. Invite the power of disruption that shakes us up and disorients us, that opens portals, seducing us towards the in-between spaces and to dance in the wild unknown. To see creation and destruction as necessary for each other's survival, and the inherent violence in what we have named nature. Let us be students of alchemy and mischief, and to think and act in unorthodox ways as the wise fool.

Perhaps this is the time for courtship—writing love letters to stones, singing ballads to the morning sun, reciting sonnets to your own wild twin. Lean in a bit closer to the trouble and wax poetry about what we find there, while we drink whiskey around a campfire. Create art, seek pleasure and bewilderment, pay attention to your dreams, make love, play, dance, find the holy in unexpected places. Offer prayers to the old gods and as we walk through this initiation of mythic proportions.

Perhaps it's time for deep remembering and reclamation. Finding wisdom in the old ways and old stories, while allowing them to breathe and change form in the world as it is, in this ever-shifting moment. To collaborate simultaneously with our ancestors and children. To sit with the many troubles of being alive, to let go of reaching towards any sort of arrival, victory, or stability, and meet each other in our differences. Let's stay shattered a while, and let ourselves spill up and out of the many containers we have confined ourselves to; never certain, never permanent, never alone, never not broken.

WOOD AND WATER

I have no interest in systems or theories or ways of navigating the world that don't come straight from the dirt. The dirt beneath the dirt. Down where ancestral bones dance with stardust and all of our composted prayers and grief. My devotion is to the subtle, the slow, the simple, the sensual that spills up and out from raw earth, meeting my mud-stained feet in an ancient courtship. Can you make a ritual out of the mundane? Show me how you compose a love song to the sacred with your bare hands and an honest heart.

Chop wood, carry water.

When is the last time you really let go? Unclenched your fists, rolled your shoulders back, softened your gaze to look beyond the bills, the scrolling, the endless to-dos and what-ifs. What is trying to dream through you? There are entire worlds at the crossroads between deep-in-your-bones knowing and wildly bewildered confusion. When curiosity meets softness and surrender, we may just be able to attune our senses to sniff out the fruit of good questions over short-sighted answers, and get so hopelessly lost that we free ourselves from the internment of arrival.

Burn wood, pour water.

What wants to be remembered, and what wants to be released? I am the acorn and the mighty oak. I am the raindrop and the vast ocean. My salt water gives libations to that which is growing, thriving, dying, decomposing. Rise,

....

swell, fall, overflow. Let's come apart and unravel, let's bleed into each other, melting into a place where sense-making finds no suitable place to assert its limited view. Can you pollinate your love with the grief that has been gathered on your soft, tender body? I came from the dirt and I will return to the dirt, each and every time I let myself burn all the way down into fertile ground.

Offer the ashes, spill your tears.

REMEMBER

We grieve
so we can love more deeply
We run away
so we can return home to ourselves
We hold on
so we can let go
We walk through fire
so we can rise from the ashes
We harden
so we can feel softness
We get lost
so we can gather the bones
We fall
so we can learn to rise
We resist
so we can surrender
We break down
so we can break open
We die many deaths
so we can be reborn
We forget
so we can remember
that this...
this too
is sacred

TAKE UP SPACE

There is a form of violence that we commit against ourselves when we make the quest for personal growth a mission to heal from our own perceived inherent flaws, which is essentially our own humanness. A mission to annihilate any parts of who we are that are hiding in the shadows, and shape-shift into a version of ourselves that finally feels deserving of love. The tools we use to self-nurture can become weapons when we are wielding them from a place of shame and unworthiness to beat our shadows into submission.

Sometimes the greatest service we can do for ourselves—for the world—is to completely fall apart, fall down to your knees, wail, and let the tears stream down your face. Forget about trying to love and light your way out of it. Let the grief or fear or sadness or trauma or anxiety take up some space. You are simply letting your humanness and wholeness take up space, because it is all there for a reason. Your deepest wound is the gateway to your greatest gift. Stand at its feet with your heart splayed out and offer it your impassioned love and gratitude. Shine light into its shadowy depths and let it be witnessed, let it breathe. Give it your attention and be a student of its precious lessons—it is an old sage with answers to your most burning questions. Ask it what it is here to teach you, and ask it what it needs to be loved. Bring it flowers and prayers and songs, sing to the cadence of your heartbeat, sing the songs of your soul bones until they flesh out with new life.

We can learn so much by looking to the cycles of death and birth—one does not exist without the other, and they both come from the same place inside of us. Taking time to sit in the darkness lets us see what is aching and yearning to be loved, what needs tending, what desires are longing to be expressed, what needs to be grieved and forgiven. It shows us the pathway to freedom. It lets us take time to be a doula of death, allowing a graceful passing of what needs to die, so we can then midwife the new life born from it.

This journey is a vigorous one, and if you need to, just rest. Refill your cup. Ask for support and know that needing it does not mean you've failed. Treat yourself with a fierce gentleness. There is something to be said for taking a big leap, but there is also something to be said for taking your time. Don't rush to throw up your sails in the winds of change if you are standing in a sinking ship. You cannot simply will your flowers to grow, and they may take more than one season to bloom. Take time to dig your hands into the dirt, work the earth, water the seeds with your sweat and tears. Be the sun, so when those leaves unfurl they will photosynthesize your own divine light to feed you.

Let yourself take up space. Let all of it take up space. Take back the power that you have given away to old stories of unworthiness, to social programming, to the myth of separation, to those who wish to keep you boxed into a shell of who you truly are. Take. Up. Space. Let yourself feel all of it, let it ravage you, right down to your core, and live your truth born from that soul place.

Rather than a final destination to grasp for, let healing be an ever-unfolding, fully felt journey.

LAY IT DOWN

You can lay down
your prayers
your art
your grief
your beauty
your tears
your sweetness
your pain
your pleasure
your rage
your sex
your love
as an offering to the divine.
It is all sacred, it is all welcome.

WINTER

...or how to die well

WINTER SOLSTICE

Winter solstice.
The rebirth of the sun
and the slow,
slow return of the light.
'Tis the season to turn inward
stoke the fires
nourish
snuggle
reflect
rest.
The time to tend our roots
that will feed the blooms
yet to come.
Sip broth of bone, fat and root
and simmer yourself right down
to the bottom of the pot.
Revel in beeswax-lit lullabies
the smell of old books
and teakettle conversations.
Tuck yourself in and hibernate
in the sweet blanket of darkness
in moonlit snow
in the long cold nights.
Take some time
to slow down and stop
doing
doing
doing
and

just be.
Undress the heaviness
from your bones
and dance with your ghosts.
Sink your teeth into this long night.
Let the moon howl at you
and slowly sing you back
from shadow
to light.

WATER WOMAN

You are the face we see
when they talk about feminine intuition.
You beckon me to come closer
with the ebb and flow of your tides
washing over me with your siren song.
You are a sea of love
with ten thousand rivers
feeding into your ocean.
A soothing cup of chamomile tea
with a dash of bourbon
to warm me all the way down.
Pull me in with the riptides of your currents
and let me learn how to swim
in your saltwater swells.
You could carve canyons with your tears
and open up the skies
with your laughter.
Try as we may to explore
the far corners of your depths
we will never be able
to reach
the bottom.

TENDING THE FIRE

I can feel the way the soft underbelly of winter makes us all a little more raw, more tender, makes us turn in a little closer to ourselves. More permission to rest, get quiet, be still. Grief sits closer to the heart and marks our face with saltwater and truth. Fewer answers, more questions. The crisp air brings clarity. Deeper gratitude for sunshine and candlelight. The patience to turn bone to broth, to chop wood and stoke fires. Warm the body with wool and whiskey, with stories and snuggles and laughter that make the oxytocin flow like honey wine. The sharp pangs of longing and desire will make the belly growl and the mind restless. More time to feel all the things that summer exuberance distracts us from. The Gregorian call for new beginnings and intention setting feels at odds with the natural rhythm to instead die a little death and stay there for a while. Wade deep in the waters of the underworld, all of our wild tendrils sinking into the subterranean as mycelium running. Emotions composting into fertile ground that puts dirt under our nails. There is a beauty in the coming undone, in the sadness, the stillness, the darkness, in the way our heavily clothed bodies become even more naked under the long cold nights, and work a little harder to tend the inner fire.

THE GIFTS OF GRIEF

If you told me two years ago that having my heart broken would take me home to myself—and help me start to fall in love with myself—I would have laughed. And by laughed, I mean that crazy, confusing kind of laugh that makes you want to avoid eye contact and back away slowly.

The relationship that I thought would last until my final breath ended, and with that, came many little deaths. The death of my future as I knew it, my life plans, my dreams, our dreams, children who would never be born, a love that once thrived. All gone. My eyes were waterfalls in the months that followed. Things like eating and taking a shower felt like monumental and unappealing tasks. I tried to keep my shit together when I ran into friends at the grocery store and explained what happened while fighting back tears in the produce aisle. I replayed and over-analyzed every moment of the last ten years of my life—of our life—trying to pinpoint where things went wrong, what was wrong with me, what was wrong with us, how he could do this to me. I felt a deep shame around the relationship ending and found it hard to reach out for support. After a while, people stop asking you if you are all right and just assume you are, because hey, it's been a whole three months, so why wouldn't you be over it by now? I told myself 'okay, this is just a breakup, people go through this all the time, I'll be fine.'

Oh, grief, how I underestimated you.

See, here's the thing about grief—when it's living inside you, there is nothing else. Its weight keeps you firmly planted in its presence with no hope for slipping away unnoticed. Sure, you can plaster a lopsided smile on your face and drag yourself to work, go about your day, and pretend to have fun, but it's always there... waiting to come crashing over you like a tsunami. That is, if you let it. Amidst the internal chaos, I still had enough awareness to know that I had two choices in front of me: I could avoid what I was feeling at all costs, taking the well-intended advice of friends and go out, date, find a hobby, anything I could to distract myself. The other option was to dive into the depths headfirst. I dove.

In hindsight, I think I only had the illusion of choice. I have always felt the full spectrum of my emotions very deeply, and there was no holding the magnitude of this back. I clumsily surfed the waves of disbelief, sadness, shame, jealousy, anger, depression, functioning as an adult in the world, trying to catch my breath... wash, rinse, repeat. I could pretend to be okay for small pockets of time, and then would let myself come completely undone.

Next, after starting to unpack my emotions around the relationship coming to an end, came one of the hardest blows yet: I HAVE NO IDEA WHO I AM. I had become quite accustomed to following someone else's lead, which conveniently allowed me to avoid asking myself lots of tough questions. Who am I? What are my gifts? What do I want? What is my work in the world? My deepest longing and desires? What bullshit of mine have I not owned and dealt with? It was easier to just stay small, crouched down in

.....
44

someone else's shadow... far from my own shadow, but more importantly, from my own light. This felt far less risky, and I could conveniently point to the outside world for all the ways I was unhappy in my life.

It was a cold, cold New England winter that first year. Still, on many days, I couldn't stand to do anything except bundle up in so many layers that I could barely walk, and head deep into the woods. There is something hauntingly beautiful about the silence and stillness of a snow covered forest. The absence of the expansiveness of summer's buzzing, chirping, gushing, juiciness allows you to pull deeply inward. It is part of the natural cycles of the seasons, and how appropriate as I was deep in a metaphorical winter myself. Syncing with the rhythms of nature, the life/death/life cycle, asks us to continually let what wants to live to bloom and thrive, and what needs to die to go back down into the humus to be transformed into fertile ground. I found a spot surrounded by tall pine trees where I would collapse and lay, cry, breathe, sing, feel the sun on my face. I offered up my rage, sadness, shame, despair, and confusion. I unleashed every incoherent thought and frantic emotion that surfaced.

As the days and months went on, I noticed that I felt fully witnessed, seen and heard... I felt loved and gently held by the forest, by the earth herself. It was an unconditional, tough love—the kind of motherly love that held me, soothed me, sang me a sweet song and then said 'okay darling, enough of this, now pick yourself back up and keep going.'

As time went on, something started happening... a remembrance. It was not a matter of finding myself, but of remembering that which was already deep in my bones. When you start to catch glimpses of yourself—the real you—you know it. The voice of your inner knowing, your intuition, sounds and feels much different from the cruel voices of your inner critic that you may be accustomed to hearing. It can also reveal some harsh truths—looking back at my relationship was different from this angle. I started to unclench my fists and let go of blaming him, and blaming myself, for everything that had gone wrong... I saw the role I played, the patterns I held, the wounds I had weaponized. We really didn't do anything wrong, and it couldn't have been any different... we loved each other (and still do), we did our best, and he was brave to do what he did in the end. I started to realize that the only person who is truly responsible for my happiness is me, and oh my, had I been neglecting myself. It was time for me to take a hard look at the parts of myself I had been avoiding for so long (really, for my entire life), lick my wounds, and finally learn what it means to heal.

I began to feel an unfurling—like the petals of my soul had the space to stretch out and bloom for the first time. This is a process, almost two years later, that is still in motion. Self-care has become not only a priority, but an art form. What do I need today, in this moment? What feels good to me, now? What needs to thrive, and what needs to die? I needed to let go of all the ways I thought self-care was supposed to look. I let my body move in the ways that it wants to. I let myself like —maybe even start to love—the parts of myself that had always felt weak, unworthy, and like they are just not enough. I have started the process of dismantling the stories and programs that have always dictated the way I move through the world, and the conditioning of my mind and body. I let myself look in the mirror and appreciate what I see. I practice not having shame for this new love that has been blossoming between me, myself and I. There is something about the raw, tender vulnerability of exploring these places that is utterly exhilarating. I am careful to keep my fingers on the pulse of my wild, inner knowing... if something doesn't feel like a full-bodied yes, then it is just going to have to be a no. I am still learning, still seeking, still healing, still growing.

There is a Japanese art form called *kintsukuroi* or *kintsugi* which translates loosely to 'mending with gold.' Pottery that has been broken is put back together with gold or silver, illuminating the beauty in the broken places. The heart is much like this... it breaks, it's messy, and it's never the same again. But it comes back together healed, stronger, more beautiful than before, alchemized by the light that fills the cracked spaces. There is something lovely about a heart that has never been broken—it is sweet, soft, and innocent. But oh, a heart that has been smashed to pieces... one that has been blasted open and made whole again, piece by piece, with the finest gold... one that has been tenderized yet made strong... the light spilling out is nearly blinding. May we all emerge from our deepest pain more beautiful, more whole, and more luminous than we ever dreamed was possible.

FEEL IT ALL

Can you sit with this ocean of grief?
Can you feel the gravity of what is happening
without rushing towards silver linings
or happy endings?
Let the wound bleed a little longer
without running to cauterize it
with certainty or guarantees.
Let the lacerations cut a little deeper
carving lessons of the great mystery
into your flesh
and lean in close
to the pain.
Can you soothe without numbing?
Feel the deep and raw somatic sensations
that swell and ooze
through each subtle body layer.
Paint new landscapes with your frayed nerves
as your tongue searches for words
in a language that you have never had to speak before.
Feel the searing truth that nothing is certain
not today
or tomorrow
not the very next breath.
It never was
but in this moment
we cannot ignore that.
Death sits close right now
we have a front row seat
to the cycles

....

of living and dying.
Feel the shakiness of your trust
the gnawing fear
the sting of loss
the burning anger
the confusion leaving you grasping
for why
and how
and when will this end?
Dissolve into the still point
beyond thinking and doing
and feel the exquisite ache
of the heartbreaking
heart-opening act
of surrender.

DEER MEDICINE

I hit and killed a deer on my way home last night, our worlds colliding at one very precise moment in time. Those who know me well know that this is not the kind of thing that my sensitive nervous system typically handles in a skillful way. I flinched and closed my eyes on impact, and when I opened them I didn't see the deer within my frazzled field of vision. I drove the last few minutes home trembling before turning back to find it, laying my hand on her soft, lifeless body and saying a prayer. There was guilt and grief, and also an unusually calm clarity.

As humans, there is always death just beyond our fingertips—on our dinner plates, below our feet, keeping our bodies warm, fueling our various wants and needs—but we are often so far removed that we do not have any kind of relationship with it. There is an intimacy at the precipice of life and death that brings the veil very thin, and creates a deeper well to acknowledge, take responsibility, offer gratitude, and grieve. To let it take up space in your heart and feel into the greater cycles that are constantly turning, the aliveness and sentience in everything around us, shimmering at the outer edges of our vision. There is power in giving and taking life that deserves our full attention and reverence—the power of creation and destruction is woven into the fabric of our collective being, and we do a great disservice to ourselves by pulling our threads out of the tapestry.

It is not lost on me that there are always messages below the surface, and shared contracts being fulfilled. The deer folk have always come to me with reminders of grace, ease, and gentleness, with their sweet innocence, and it is interesting that we would come together in this intimately violent way. I also notice this comes at a time when the archetype of the sweet good girl has been dying a slow death inside of me, and may very well be meeting her ultimate and swift end as we speak. I also know, simultaneously, that this did not happen *for* me, and none of it means anything. But there is always sticky sweet medicine dripping from every sacred and profane exchange, and I will always choose to drink up every last drop.

HER

When you speak her name
does she know
how long
my own name
dripped from your tongue?

SOFTER

Go softly.
Softer.
Softer, still.
We're all in the belly of the beast now
so find a place to lay your head down
and sink deep into the thick velvet
of your animal body.

What happens now?
Now that the ghosts of the machine
have haunted the halls of purity
wrapped in their flags and audacity
chanting manifestos of violence
and the monster
has finally started
to devour itself.

I see you praying to Jesus
when what you need is Baba Yaga
and the old trickster gods
of your wayback people.
I see you venerating the Virgin
when there is no innocence left
inside porcelain flesh
and we all come from the soft wet folds
of a woman.

So what now?
Now that we've forgotten how to show up

with blood, bone, and grit at the table
ready with
courage of heart
willingness to repair
impeccable with our words
and accountable in our actions.

Fine tune your tongue
to speak the dialect of a body
that has chosen to be whole
and eat the seeds of longing
that will plant a lion's roar in your throat.
Breathe in, breathe out;
the oscillation between
the truth that sits inside your ribcage
and the words that leave your lips.
Will they be violent?
Will they be loving?
How else could you possibly express
who you are
if not by how you choose to live?

Pull yourself up to the fire
and ready your quiver
sharpen your vision
and gather your tools:
The old myths and stories,
so you remember what to do.
A pinch of mugwort in your pocket,
to walk you through the dreamtime.

Rosewater,
to cool the fire.
A spell scrolled on birch bark,
to stoke it.
A heart song,
so the moon knows how to find you.

Beauty will still have it's way with us
while we make space
for grief
and anger
and sadness
and rest
and laughter
and play
and tears
and grace
and joy
and right action.

It's your move, sweet thing.
Do not lose heart
listen closely
remember who you are
and take the very next step
that's right in front of you.

UNPACKING

To the women: I love you. I want to love you with my whole, cracked-open heart. I want to support you. I don't know how.

To the men: I love you. I want to love you with my whole, cracked-open heart. I want to support you. I don't know how.

Women, you are bleeding. Your first blood came long ago, not from between your legs but as you clenched your jaw, biting hard onto your tongue, with unspoken words dripping down your chin. Who do you think you are, speaking, thinking, feeling for yourself? Be a nice girl. You swallowed so many emotions that the only thing that survived was bitterness and fear.

Men, you are bleeding. Your first blood came long ago when you were told to be a man, show no fear or weakness, and you beat your heart into a pulp until it bled out. You were told your emotions had no place, no right, to live inside you because real men don't cry, so stop being such a pussy. You swallowed so many emotions that the only thing that survived was numbness and anger.

Women, you have hurt me. You have cut me down with the sharpness of your words... those spoken to me, and those that were daggers into my back. You called me a slut when I consented, and a slut when I didn't consent. You have competed with me, and wished for me to fail to gain the attention of men. You have shamed my body, my words, and the paths I have chosen. You have torn me down with envy to feel your value at the expense of my own. You have disregarded the monogamy of my relationships to satisfy your conquests, and you enjoyed being the woman on the side. You have bullied and abused me. You have reminded me that I have failed my duties as a woman by not being a wife and mother. You have played your role in upholding rape culture when you protect and defend predators, when you place blame on your sisters, when you slut shame and dehumanize. You have deepened the gender divide, and the old stale gender roles and conditioning of the patriarchy.

Men, you have hurt me. You have talked down to me, talked over me, talked about and to me like I was an object. You have been violent with your words and actions. You have called me a slut for giving sex, and a tease when I have not. You have tried to possess me as one of your belongings. You have made decisions about me and my body that I did not condone, because you didn't think I had any right to have a say in it. You have reminded me again and again that I am not safe in this body, and of all the ways I could 'ask for it.' You have asserted your strength over me because you saw me as a conquest... or inhuman... or both. You have imprinted the trauma of generations and generations of burning and rape and abuse along my ancestral bloodlines, and I can feel the pain and grief and fear of these wounds deep in my bones and nervous system.

Women, I have hurt you, too. I have hurt you in so many of the ways you have hurt me. My feminism has neglected indigenous women, black women, women of color, queer women, and trans women. My feminism has not made room for you to forgive and heal. I have watched you make yourself smaller to make me more comfortable in the way that I have for you. I have perpetuated the sister wound over and over again.

Men, I have hurt you, too. I have been angry with you for not giving me what I wanted from you even though I never told you what that was. I have expected you to always know exactly what to say and do, to remain stoic in the face of my chaos, to 'be a man.' I expected you to be strong for me, even though no one was being strong for you. I have been angry that you could not hear the words I was afraid to speak or feel into the pain I could not express. I have dismissed you with 'that's just how men are,' deepening the shaming of the masculine. I have been afraid of you and angry with you because of things another man did. I have forgotten all the times throughout history that you were sent to war, that you had to watch as your women were burned and raped, that you were expected to provide at all costs, that you were not allowed to feel or express any of it, that you had to turn to destructive ways of coping again and again. I didn't notice that you are so much more likely to be murdered, to commit suicide, and that, still, male genital mutilation is still normalized. I didn't see your pain, and I didn't stand up for you.

Women, oh you have LOVED me. You have shown me the many faces of the feminine: the sovereignty of the Maiden, the creative force and nurturing of the Mother, the deep wisdom of the Crone. You have taught me about the nature of creation and destruction through the Wild Woman and the Dark Goddess. You have shown me the freedom to express sensuality and sexuality as the Lover, and the strength and prowess of the Huntress. Sisters, you are all of this and more… I bow deeply to your grace, your strength, your softness, and your resilience. You have helped me remember how to be in devotion to the Old Ways, and what it means to pray. You have been a soft shoulder to cry on and a deep listening ear. You have shown me how to receive. You have inspired me to know that I can do anything, be anything, if I only dare to. You have shown me the true meaning of sisterhood. You have taught me who I am—you have been a mirror that reflects back all the gifts, beauty and strength I could not see in myself.

Men, oh how you have LOVED me. You have shown me the many faces of the masculine: the courage and strength of the Warrior, the warm, loving care of the Father, the steadiness and integrity of the King. You have loved all of me from an endless well as the Lover, and you have made love to me. Brothers, you are all of this and so much more… I bow deeply to your strength, your wisdom, to the full spectrum of all that lives inside you. You have shown me the most tender vulnerability, the depth of love in your heart, and you have trusted me to receive it. You have shown me the beautiful alchemy that occurs when the masculine and feminine merge into one. You have made me feel safe in my skin, safe in the world, safe to express who I am, safe to fall apart, safe to speak my desires. You taught me how to surrender, how to lead, how to take action. You have shown me how someone who has carried a heavy weight on their shoulders can still stand tall. You have taught me who I am—you have been a mirror that reflects back all the gifts, beauty and strength I could not see in myself.

To the women: I love you. I want to love you with my whole, cracked-open heart. I want to support you. Please teach me how.

To the men: I love you. I want to love you with my whole, cracked-open heart. I want to support you. Please teach me how.

THE FALSE SELVES

We can so easily become addicted
to the games we play
in order to collect tiny morsels of acceptance.

These are futile games
of measuring risk and reward
clenching your fists
around the reins that tame your wild heart.

Carefully calculating
every word that escapes your lips
every emotion that seeps through your pores
every move your body makes
squeezing them all into a tiny box
that gives the illusion of safety.

There is a hunger for this kind of safety and security
that requires feverish effort to sustain.

How can you mold yourself into what is
lovable
acceptable
and what you believe
makes everyone else more comfortable?

What lies do you need to tell yourself
and everyone around you
to stay small?

We abandon and reject ourselves
in attempt to prevent
being abandoned and rejected by others
and call it love.

This is not love.
This is not nourishment.
You are throwing scraps to the hungry wolves inside you
and they are ready to devour you.
Can you even feel yourself anymore?

After creating the minefield of all the things
you can and cannot say
the things you can and cannot feel
and still be deemed worthy
what is left of you?

You've traded your wholeness
for a fractured caricature of a good person.

You cannot outrun who you truly are
you cannot will yourself into a healed state
and you are dying a slow death by trying.

How safe do you feel now?
Now that you know you've been plotting your own
execution?
What will you do about it?

You cannot clean a wound
with the blood that has been spilled

.....

nor can you wipe your tears
when you are alone
and drowning in their salty waters.

Build a funeral pyre for every version of yourself that is not
the Truth;
the nice one
the unworthy one
the wounded one
the accommodating one
the victimized one
the appropriate one
every one that wears a distorted mask
and suffocates you with each passing day.

Light it with the fire in your belly
that you so carefully contain
the fire in your eyes
that you've tried to dim
the fire in your heart
that is burning with and for love.

Invite everyone you love
to dance around the fire with you
with bare feet
and open hearts.

Say a prayer
and watch them burn
down to a pile of ashes.

Feel it tearing you into pieces
then watch the Phoenix spread her fiery wings.
String the bones left behind around your neck
to remind you
of what death feels like
and what birth feels like.

Remember who you are
and remember to die
whenever you need
so that you may live.

TO MY HEART

My dear heart, you need tending. I am grateful for your resilience and your patience, for your unwavering presence in the chest of my soul through all that you have endured. I vow my devotion to you now… to listen to you, to trust you, to set you free.

I will forgive myself for letting harm come to you, and for holding on to the pain of others so tightly. For letting you drown in the grief of the world. For the conscious and unconscious agreements I made to try and keep you safe. For the ways I have separated myself from you and abandoned you. For the carefully constructed fortress I built up around you that did not actually hold any clear or safe boundaries.

I will dismantle the walls that surround you, brick by brick, and I will not punish myself for building them in the first place. I will give you safe space to heal—from the wounds of lovers, of self-flagellation, of the grief that comes with being human. From the witch's wound that told me I would die from speaking what is written on your walls.

I will build an altar before you and leave offerings of prayer and laughter, of song and the movement of my body. I will feed you with sunshine and moonlight, water and earth. I will surround myself with people who honor you. I will tend, nurture, and align myself to you. I will make space for the desires that live inside you to be birthed into my awareness, and I will let them be free and heard and seen when I come to know them. I will trust that I am worthy of these desires, that I can ask for them, and that I can receive their manifestations.

I will overcome my fear of letting you be open for the world to see. I will not be ashamed for wanting to be open to you, for wanting you to be open to others, for wanting the exchange of love to flow freely to and from you. I will let you love and break and mend and love, over and over again. I want to live from your center and feel you flow to my fingertips, to my mouth, down to my feet. Let me speak and feel and walk in your light.

I will come to embody the understanding that when I open to you, a reservoir of truth and love is birthed and can flow freely. That this is how the divine speaks and breathes and lives within and through me while I walk in this sacred vessel of a body. That this is how the love and wisdom of my ancestors speak to and through me. I will trust this holy language, and I will let myself be a conduit for it to channel through. I will tether my voice to you with a golden thread.

I will no longer seek safety through trying to silence or control you. I will risk pain and grief for truth, whether or not it will be received or returned to me, and will allow myself to feel all that you have the capacity to let me feel. I will trust that the amount of love that can flow from you and be received by you is not scarce or limited. I will remember that the deepest grief is a reflection of the depth of my love, and I will accept the beautiful gifts that you bring me in both the light and the darkness. I will see the duality of your humanness and your divinity, and surrender to all of it. I will find comfort in the discomfort of deepening further into the vulnerability that this requires.

I will honor your soft nudges and your rallying cries. Your longing and your pain. I will lean in close and listen to the quietest whispers. I will meet your aches with even more love. I will remember that you are my holy compass, and return back to you each time I forget. I will follow the path that you lay out before me, even when I can't yet see where it leads.

And my dear heart, I am terrified, but I see no other way. I have tried to keep you safe and locked away for too long. You have the floor now... I am listening.

BOW

Maybe it's time to learn to bow
to the darkness.
To befriend the shadows
that sit unnoticed
in the forgotten corners
of your being.
Let your Sunday morning hymn
sing the sadness in your body
to the light in your eyes
and know that both
bring a bounty of teachings
to your soft and tender heart.

LOVE AND GRIEF

What if grief and love are the same?
Perhaps grief is the container
and we can only love as much as grief can hold.
A cavern carved deep into the chest
echoing with the emptiness where love has lived
and was lost
and will live again.
Broken hearts are cracked wide open
stitched back together with grace and gratitude
able to hold deeper depth
and greater capacity.
The courage required to love
is the same
as the courage required to grieve.
The enormity of it all
a force that cannot be controlled or predicted
and demands to remain messy
and free of any language that tries to define it.
Tears, and more tears, and more tears
because you are water
and there in an ocean inside you
marking your face with salt
and memories of the happiest of times.
Flowers, for all the beauty and joy and warmth
and for the fragility and impermanence of it all.
A lump in the throat
that holds all the was expressed
and all that went unspoken.
I'm sorry, please forgive me, thank you, I love you.

The gravity of sadness
that keeps you tethered to the earth
and lets you appreciate the weightlessness
of pure joy.
An alchemy of the soul
all the ash left behind
becoming fertile soil and rich humus
watered with tears and resilience
fed with prayers and laughter
opening, widening, expanding
into what now has space
to bloom.

BOUNDARIES

My heart
and my body
are not battlefields
for you to wield your weapons
gathered from every war
you lost
before me.

TO MY FELLOW CHILDLESS QUEENS

I know that ache in your womb.
The blueprints laid out on the altar of your heart
with the most exquisite architecture
that may never meet hands to build it.

I know the thunder of your longing.
A sound that is slowly drowned out
by the ticking of a clock
that reminds you that 'someday' may never come.

I know the way their words puncture you.
The questions of why not and when
and don't you want to be a mother?
The rancid balm of canned responses
bereft of any empathy.
The way you offer up politeness
stained in blood from biting your tongue
when the truth tastes more like
I tried
I can't
I lost it
I'm out of time
I don't want to.

I see the Mother in you.

The Creatrix who can birth an entire universe
with prayers that slip through red-stained lips
with words to paper

with paintbrush to canvas
with the swaying of hips that remind us
of where we came from.

There is life-giving magic
between your thighs
that can create new worlds
and set them all on fire.

Your hands drip with the honey
of a loving touch
that could soothe the sting of heartache
and repair the deepest soul-wound.

There is a sword at your tongue
an entire lineage in your spine
armed with the wisdom and power
to protect all that you love.

You are an Ancestor
writing stories in your womb
flowers blooming from your tender heart
seeds planted beneath your feet
watered with your tears and your joy.
You are the Earth embodied
with a fire in your belly
and a thousand rivers flowing through your veins
feeding into the ocean of your love.

I want you to know
that everything born
from the sacred and holy ground
of your heart
is a gift to this world
and it will live on
through everything
and everyone
and every heart
you touch.

BOUNTY

I hear there's a bounty on my womb.
A high price in the currency
of power and control.
In the currency
of violence
and cowardice.

You want to make a home in this body.
Penetrate it with your power and lust
and demand I carry the seed you've planted
pretending to protect the sacred
when we both know
your concern is for birth
and not for life.
I've seen the way you watch
as young mouths go unfed
as young arms are torn from their mother's embrace
as young bodies are raped and ravaged and locked away
in the land of the free
and home of the brave.

You read me ghost stories
from the good book
about purity
and innocence
and all the ways my body is wrong
and all the ways my body
does not belong to me.
But I prefer different fairy tales.

The ones that were woven from an
ancient mother's womb
whispered to her from deep in the earth.
The ones that teach me
that I am fire and water
that I am land and thunder
that I am holy and sacred
that I am the great creator and destroyer
that I belong to me
and only me
and I alone
will decide.

I hear there's a bounty on my womb
but you seem to forget
that I am the huntress
and I can smell the fear
dripping from your cowardly words
and I dare you to try and hold my fire
in your bare, trembling hands.

SPRING

...or how to bloom

SPRING EQUINOX

Waking from the strange dreams of winter slumber
and sliding into the psychedelic textures
of this glorious balance
between night and day
light and dark.
Rub your sleepy eyes awake
open them wide
to the exalted enchantment of this
fragile, wild, messy, exquisitely beautiful
waking world.
Sink into the remembrance
born from death.
Let your bare feet touch the thawing Earth
get some dirt under your nails
and let the sun kiss your cheeks.
Flirt with the subtle layers
and the expansive wildness.
Let the song of a bird
the warmth of the air
the budding of trees
the rumble of thunder
all bring you
right down to your knees
in devotion.
Let your heart blossom and bloom
unfurling from your chest
pouring in every direction
out into the cosmic, playful, lustful dance of life.

Offer up your lovemaking as a prayer
while the
buzzing
buzzing
buzzing of bees
will soon have sticky sweet honey
dripping down the thighs of the Earth mother
ripe with the scent of flowers
and of sex and creation.
We are all alive, together, now.
What beauty are you ready to birth?

AIR WOMAN

Tell me stories with the prowess
of your serpent tongue
and make love to my mind
as you weave the words
that seduce your lungs.
There are entire philosophies in your eyes
written by the ancients.
Penetrate me with your deep knowing
that will open up the skies to the gods
with your crack of thunder
that reverberates through every corner of me.
I know the owls share their secrets with you
under the soft light of the moon;
sing them to me with your wood thrush song
in the soft light of the morning sun.
You caress my skin like a cool breeze
with the softest kiss on the nape of my neck
but I'd be a fool if I didn't remember
how easily you can level me
with your storm.

HEALING IN RELATIONSHIP

We were never meant to do any of this alone. Not our joy, our grief, our rage, our deepest expression of love. We weren't meant to try and process our personal and collective pain and trauma on our own. We are not supposed to live without touch, without gazing into each other's eyes, without the warmth of each other's presence, without long conversations that end in an embrace. We cannot remember who we are if our bare feet don't touch the earth, if we are not in relationship with the land.

In some ways, we are more connected than ever, with the world quite literally at our fingertips through the touch of a screen. At the same time, we have never been so separate and lonely. As someone who has always walked the line between being introverted and isolated, my increasingly virtual world has been both a saving grace and a sneaky enabler. I can feel a form of connection, interaction, and a sense of feeling witnessed in my expression, and I can learn—through a narrow lens—about what is going on in the world... but it is all from a very safe distance. Words and photos are carefully curated, and lack the depth that occurs when two bodies are in each other's field, feeling into one another. Feedback is not immediate—I can't feel the pain, joy, confusion or arousal that I invoke in someone's body, and they cannot feel mine if I am afraid to express it. I am left feeling simultaneously full and completely empty.

The narrative that tells us that self-love and self-care are all we need to be healed and whole is doing a great disservice to humanity at large, because it is only a partial truth. To be sure, these two practices are essential and build important foundations for our wellbeing—it is important to know how to be alone, to love yourself fiercely, to lay down boundaries that create the kind of safety that allows you to connect and love freely. But these are only strands of a much wider web. I have struggled my way through some really heavy shit, all alone, and likely dragged everyone around me through my muck in the process. We need self-care, yes, but we also need community care.

Healing happens in relationship. The relationship could be with our own body, with lovers, with a river, with friends and family, with an illness, with plant medicine, with literally every person we encounter. Relationships challenge us in ways that all the meditation and flower baths and cancelled plans could ever do. They hold up a mirror to show us what we cannot see on our own—what needs tending, what wounds are still oozing in unmetabolized pain. They can hold us with grace and love while we fall apart, and provide safe space to mend.

I have felt the medicinal balm of sitting with a tree, a dear friend, in sacred circle, and dancing wildly amidst sweaty bodies. I learned volumes about myself from lovers who have held me with tender reverence, and ones who did not. I hear the whispers of my ancestors, the spirits of the land, the messengers in the dreamtime who all help light my path. Illness has taught me to rest when I need to. Being witnessed in my sadness, anger, confusion, pleasure, tears, in my wild beautiful and messy expression, is a baptism. I am feeling the way that letting my walls down is allowing in exquisite connection. I still, in part, hold the belief that letting all of me be fully seen will result in total rejection. I've been testing these waters lately, opening, expanding, pulling back the curtains... and being lovingly accepted by some truly beautiful humans. Even still, I keep thinking that it won't last, maybe they are just being polite, maybe when I go a layer deeper they will finally leave... but there is always someone ready to show up, hold space, support, and reflect.

Let's help each other through this wild ride of life. Can we witness and hold space for others in their fully embodied expression of raw emotions, and expand our capacity to touch our own deepest grief and love? Can we say how we feel, now? Don't put off saying I love you, I need support, I appreciate you, I'm angry, I'm lonely, I need to talk. Let us open the pathways inside of us to let our fullest expression move through our bodies, and hold each other in these tender places.

MOTHER

Do you remember the sound
of the hips that cracked
to birth you
echoing all the way back
to the First Mother?

The ten thousand secrets
whispered into your blood
by every woman
that came before you.

The blessings of your lineage:
how to know yourself
how to live a life
how to heal.

The burdens:
how to hold your tongue
how to carry your pain
how to pass it on.

You look just like your mother's mother's mother
when the sun hits your face
and her voice slips through your lips
when you stand firm-footed
and say:
I remember.

You look just like your daughter's daughter's daughter
when the moon reflects in your eyes
and her voice drips from your tongue
when you stand firm-footed
and say:
this ends with me.

Don't you realize
that you can midwife your own birth
as often as you need to?

Listen closely
to the pulse of silence
in the deep velvet of your womb
until you hear a gentle voice
that whispers
'this is the way.'

REFLECTION

Bring me your pain, your sorrow, your despair.
I will show you your resilience;
a vibrant rainbow after a turbulent storm.

Bring me your sharp edges.
I will show your your soft curves.

Bring me your fear, your quivering lip, your desire to run.
I will show your your strength, your courage, your ability to
stand firmly rooted.

Bring me your wounds.
I will show your strong, mended heart
pieced together with the finest gold.

Bring me your messiness and chaos.
I will show you your beauty and calm inner waters.

Bring me your darkness and shadows.
I will show you your extraordinary light.

Bring me your shame and timidness.
I will show your wild, your free, your sensual and sexual
nature.

Bring me your grief.
I will show you the depth of your love.

Bring me all that you thought
you had ever lost.
I will show you
that it was always there
waiting for you
kept safely in your heart.

A BLESSING

May you be well in body, mind and spirit
May you be joyful
May you be free from harm and from harming others
May you feel safe in your body
May you have space to rest
May you have space to play
May you be free to feel all of your feelings
May you be nourished by pleasure
May your voice be met with kind and receptive ears
May your grief be a testament to how deeply you love
May your life be a testament to the light of your spirit
May you feel the protection of your ancestors' prayers
May you trust in the wisdom of your body
May you know that the love you have given was never wasted
May you receive the abundance of love that is available to you
May you love freely and deeply
May you be love

OPENING

I am interested in what is real, and honest, and all the ways we can lean in a little closer to ourselves. The way that the truth weaves softer textures into each inhale and exhale, expanding and stretching and calling us into our fullest expression.

I can feel the way so many of us have been searching for translations in a grief-illiterate culture, the ways we hide who we really are and what we really feel. The way we walk around each day without ever really seeing each other; the juxtaposition of being in a room full of people yet completely alone. A deep ache for belonging and release and connection that does not ask us to numb what is alive for us at any given moment.

Let me sit in circle for lifetimes with the ones who hold me as I wring grief from my skin, extract apologies from my spine, and scream so loud and with such ferocity that you can see the teeth marks on the anger that once lived inside my belly. The ones who witness without fixing. The ones who can see all of me and not look away.

I am all of me and all of you.
I am victim and perpetrator.
I am oppressed and oppressor.
I am maiden, mother and crone.
I am the good girl and the diabolical whore.
I am student and teacher.
I am a needy child and an evil dictator.
I am sweet nurturer and raging bitch.

....

90

I am woman, animal, and earth.

I want to never stop feeling the discomfort of sitting with pain, yours and mine, and being witnessed by the eyes and hearts of community. To be naked and raw under the glare of the gods, and claw my way back into the womb of the sacred.

I want to have the courage to speak the words that tighten my chest, and permission to be with complete silence.

I want to dance and be danced wildly in the cathedral of my body, meeting skin and muscle and unhinged primal movements with the saltwater of sweat and tears.

I want to speak my truth to you in elegant prose and in tearful incoherent sentences until we are both so uncomfortable that we crack wide open.

I want to love fully and wildly with reckless abandon and be ravished by love with no expectation. To love and lose and love again and be made better for it, more tender. To let my heart, broken or whole, cover ever-widening terrains.

At the end of it all, when you finally slip out of your soft animal body, what will your legacy be?
Did you live and love well, and fully?
Did you allow yourself to see and be seen?
Did you learn how to listen?
Did you remember who you are?

Did you catch every last drop of awe and ecstasy on your tongue and let it drip down your chin?

SAFE SPACE

Reclaiming this body as safe space.
It will not house the legacies
of silence and oppression
that came before me.
There is no room
for the cruelty of my mind
to prey on my body.
I will tend this fire in my belly.
I will speak with my serpent tongue.
You will know
the flavor of my essence
the scent of my bloom
the depth of
my devotion
my power
my holy rage
my sex
my love.
I will accept nothing less
than a full descent
into the living embodiment
of all of me.

WISH LIST

I want to make you feel something.

I want good questions to always outweigh the answers that try to meet them, just enough so that we stay curious.

I want to be guided by elders and children at the threshold of all that is both ancient and brand new.

I want ceremonies and rituals marked with fire for transitions and beginnings and endings.

I want a man to know the deepest corners of my heart as well as he knows the scent of the nape in my neck.

I want to witness you in your messy and beautiful humanness.

I want it to mean something when we say 'I love you' and when we ask 'how are you?'.

I want to let you see my inner storms that I don't like to show to anyone, and still find you standing there when the dust settles.

I want to sing you a lullaby so sweet that you can hardly bear it, and then listen while you tell me your dreams over a morning cup of tea.

I want my heart to break daily so I can piece it back together with the finest gold.

I want to cook you food that I grew with my hands and watch you lick your lips in nourishment and delight and the satiety of good company.

I want to penetrate you with my truth, delivered with a gentle and loving ferocity, and I don't want to caretake the discomfort that it makes you feel.

I want—no—I need to believe we can remember our own humanity and see ourselves in each other.

I want us to slow down.

I want to bloodlet the colonial narratives from our veins until we are forced to write new stories and remember the old ones.

I want us to see our relatives in trees and creeks and dirt and stars and in the many different human bodies.

I want you to feel safe.

I want our unlearning to be in equal measure to our new growth.

I want to trade hashtags and status updates for community care and deep listening.

I want us to remember who our Mother is and feed her with beauty and sweetness and the libation of our tears.

I want you to know that resting and grieving are a worthy use of your time.

I want us to find sanctuary in each other.

I want to live in a world where love and gratitude and compassion are the currency that we value, a world beyond our wildest imaginations, and I want us to get busy dreaming.

FLOWER EATER

Sometimes I like to eat flowers
just so I remember what it feels like
to push up through the dirt
and taste the sky.
Birthed from a love affair
between sunshine and honeybees
serenaded by the nightingale's song
and kissed by the morning dew.
Photosynthesize light
into nourishment
simply by being
so I can feed you
the sweetest nectar
and bear the fruits of joy
from my fingertips.
Unfurl and bloom
into a mighty beauty
that can bend and sway
to withstand the storm
and at the same time
disarm you
with the sweetest
and gentlest
softness.

INNER CHILD

I keep an old picture of my five-year-old self, and it makes me so happy to look at it. An old soul in a new body, eyebrows furrowed in sharp focus, likely deep in an adventure of my own imagination, bare feet on the earth, and who needs pants in the sandbox? I was wide-eyed and curious, open-hearted yet shy, joyful, playful, inquisitive, and very sensitive.

Although my world was already being shaped, this was long before life had its way with me, and a million mouths told me who I was supposed to be, what it meant to be a woman, what is right and wrong, what emotions to express or tuck away. There have been many paper cuts, and few deep gashes along the way.

Now, many years later and many miles travelled, all I want to do is forgive every version of myself between she and I so I can get back to her and love her. Her tender, loving heart still beats in my chest, her fire still flickers in my eyes. I want to offer her the wisdom I have collected that will keep her safe, and ask her for the wisdom that she has not yet forgotten. I want to let her show me how to let joy and curiosity lead the way, and see the world through her optimistic eyes. She reminds me to laugh or cry whenever I want or need to. She reminds me to stay close to the earth, and that I don't need an intermediary to talk to Spirit. I know life is short—she knows I am limitless.

You're doing good, kid. Keep going.

RECLAIM

To the Earth
To the Waters
To the Ancestors of my blood, of my Spirit, and of this land
To throwing up sails in the winds of change
To feeling it all
To letting go under the New Moon
To the Feminine
To the Masculine
To the power of human connection
To not knowing
To fucking up and trying again
To abundance
To saying yes, and to saying no
To taking care of self
To the many pathways of pleasure
To receiving
To remembrance
To reclamation

TEND

I have invested so much time, money and energy into healing myself, sometimes with such ferocity that is contradicts the very thing I am seeking. So often I have treated my mind and body as something that needs fixing, a problem to be solved, searching desperately for the tools to annihilate the issue by any means necessary. I have pushed myself to the outer edges of sanity and exhaustion with practices of self-flagellation disguised as spiritual growth and development. I've reached desperately for more pills, more retreats, more practices, more specialists, more ceremonies, more certifications, to help me finally cross some sort of imaginary finish line. There is always, inevitably, spirals of shame that come with all of this —what is *wrong* with me?

This kind of thinking does little more than dehumanize myself, yet it has followed me through depression and anxiety, chronic illness, processing heartache and grief, and trying to reconcile my sensitivity. We walk around with so many narratives and constructs about what it looks like to walk the path to healing, whether it be through the lens of allopathic medicine or alternative and spiritual traditions. There is so often a quality of numbing, dissociation, bypassing, personalizing, or blaming involved depending on which path is taken. But what if instead of trying to avoid the pain, or punishing ourselves for what we may have done to deserve this, we lean in with curiosity and receptivity? We can find meaning in each pleasurable and agonizing moment just as they are, without taking any of it personally. The drive to heal, as if it were some ultimate destination to arrive to, estranges us from our own grief and pain, and from the excruciating beauty of having our hearts broken wide open by the unforeseen visitors we encounter; be they illness, trauma, or any number of wounds that ache for us to tend.

To tend is not to fix. Tending requires an exquisite gentleness and uncompromising softness. A kindness and compassion that we may never have given ourselves the courtesy to embody before. It is a salve that cools the hot gaping wound and reminds us of the expansive landscape that lies within us. It does not ask us to answer the why that we often so desperately search for, but instead to be present with what is —not what was, what could be, or what we think should be.

Illness and wellness are not binary opposites, our inner terrains are far more complex and luscious and vast than that. There is deep pain and wounding that come with being human, and no matter how privileged or gifted or special you are, there is no escaping that. And rather than asking how can I solve this problem, and reaching for tools that promise a quick fix, what if we ask: how can I love this part of me a little more? How can I tend with grace and fierce compassion? How can I gather the strength to soften into the places where it hurts the most? How can I listen to the somatic flow of wisdom that is pouring from my being?

Take a breath. And another. Slow down. Take permission to give yourself time and space to feel your body and listen deeply to what it is telling you. Our bodies cannot be bullied into a state of health—they ask us for patience, our full attention, presence, and loving care. The wounding of our inner child can not be handled with rough, violent hands; it calls us to be the most loving parent we could possibly imagine, with a soft touch and sweet lullabies on our tongue.

We are made up of extraordinary light and darkness, and there will inevitably be cracks in the foundation that we collect along the way as our hearts and minds and bodies break over and over again. Some chasms run deep within our bloodlines and have been passed on again and again, waiting until someone finally has the capacity to tend to them. But no matter how deep the spaces, whether they be a small rift or a vast canyon, we can break and tend and radiate until we are a wondrous and holy technicolor well of wisdom that only comes when we stand with all that we are, and love it fiercely with tender-hearted presence. And the more you can do that —the more you can step fully into the wholeness and truth of ALL of who you are—the more this world gets to taste your sweet and tender medicine that only you carry.

FIND ME

You can find me in the fields dancing with the fireflies.
They know the secrets to shining light into darkness.

You can find me bathing in the salty waters of the ocean.
She knows the secrets to being a safe container, to washing
away grief.

You can find me howling with the wolves.
They know the secrets to staying wild.

You can find me basking in the moonlight.
She knows the secrets of cycles, of waxing and waning, of
what to hold and what to release.

You can find me climbing up mountain peaks.
They know the secrets to standing tall with a strong
backbone.

You can find me soaking up the warmth of the sun.
He knows the secrets to staying centered, the secrets of
strength and vitality.

You can find me sleeping at the base of an oak tree.
They know the secrets to staying rooted in fertile ground
while reaching for the sky.

You can find me buzzing with the hummingbirds.
They know the secrets to finding the sweetest nectar.

You can find me lost in the beauty
of this big beautiful
wild earth
getting lost
to find myself.

WORDS

I don't think I'll ever be able to find
the right words
to express exactly what I feel
and perhaps that's how it should be.
Maybe the indescribable
wants to taste itself
in our language
but will never invite us
to the feast.
I can feel its breath
hit the back of my ribcage
and I exhale curls of smoke
after it has burned away
the last words I had left
to try and explain
what love feels like.

Maybe there's a way
we can practice untethered devotion
to ourselves
to each other
to the great mystery
to everything that lives
inside us
around us
and moving through us
without trying to
claim it
own it

define it
or tame it
to satisfy the part of us
that needs a tidy
and obedient answer.

Can the darkness see its own shadow?
Maybe when the monsters come
and disrupt my dreams
I'll get up and brew a strong pot of coffee
and we'll sit
and sip
and watch the ghosts dance on the kitchen table
and we'll all laugh about how I used to hide my eyes
underneath the covers
not knowing that all they demanded of me
was that I witness them.

Maybe I'll learn how to trust
what feels good
and make room for it to stay a while.
Pleasure for the sake of it
and awe
in reverence to beauty.
The tenderness of a smile
or the way a dew drop rolls down a blade of grass
will always correct my posture
when there's too much weight
on my shoulders
and remind me of the holy practice
of feeling joy.

......

I'm not so proper
that I can't fall apart
and I'm not so broken
that I can't stand up taller
than a mighty oak.
I remember all that I am.
Earth to body
stardust to bone
river to blood
ocean to tears
air to breath
thunder to voice
fire to spirit
ashes to earth.

Maybe there's nothing left to say.

SUMMER

...or how to thrive

SUMMER SOLSTICE

Summer. You sweaty, sexy beast.
You are a long, slow exhale
with crimson sunsets on your breath.
Tell me stories by the campfire
under sparkling night skies
while I lick blackberry jam from my fingers
and the fireflies hold council in the meadow.
Your expansive landscape
lets me stretch my quivering tendrils wide
intoxicating my senses
until I touch the outer edges
of your scintillating wildness.
Seduce me with your late afternoon thunderstorms
that roll through my body
stir my soul
and draw lightning from my fingertips.
Play me a symphony
of your raw and scorching aliveness
that sings hymns in the sunlight
and lullabies under the moon.
Let me relish in the abundance spilling over
from the pelvic bowl of the Earth Mother
while morning dew beads upon her breasts
and the sweetest nectar pours from her womb.
Baptize me in ocean waves
and warm, soft rain
in the sweat on my skin
and the thick, moist air.
Make my soft animal body supple

with your penetrating heat
like a plump red strawberry
hanging low and heavy
ready to be plucked
and savored
with my juices
dripping down your chin.

FIRE WOMAN

Keeper of the flame
the spark of creation
the blaze of transformation
and the holy fire of feminine rage.
You are every burning sunset
painted in crimson and ruby magnificence
that leaves me yearning for your dawn.
Even the mighty sequoia wants to arc
towards the warmth of your skin
just to get a taste your light.
You Phoenix.
I see that wild spark in your eyes
spitting flames with your words
as you
burn it
all
down
only to dance upon the ashes.
You are the burning passion
that stirs a warm ache between my hips
flushes my cheeks
and draws unholy prayers from my mouth.
I would be wise to just let you have your way with me.

THE WILD WILL CALL YOU BACK

The Wild will call you back.
Through half-remembered dreams
and sunsets painted
in burnt sienna
and vermillion flames
she will call you back home.
The coyotes will wake you
from your sleep
with their clarion call
to keep your eyes
wide open.

How long have you been sleeping?
How much have you forgotten?

The Wild will call you back.
She will hang you upside down
and shake the nonsense
from the pockets
of your mind.
She will strip your soul naked
leaving you raw and exposed
under the searing glare
of the gods.
Offer up the holiness
of your confusion
and questions.
Dress yourself
in fireflies

......

and attune your senses
to awe
while you learn the slow seduction
of courting your muse.

Brush the stardust from your wings
and wipe the ocean from your eyes.
Flex your claws
dig your roots deep down
into the fertile earth
and show your fangs.
Gather pollen on your legs
and speak
in venom
and honey.
Peel back your colonized tongue
and let it hiss
and purr
and growl
and scream.

Do you remember
how to stalk
as predator
and how to surrender
as prey?

The Wild will call you back.
The owls know your real name
and will call you

from the darkness of night
to dance under the moon.
Crack your heart open
with your ancestors' bones
and dance in the ecstasy
of your love
and your grief
with flailing limbs
bloody knees
and mud-stained feet.
Braid mugwort into your hair
and dream yourself
awake.

The Wild will call you back.
She will teach you how to die
again and again
and how to die well.
There is no difference
between your funeral pyre
and your birth canal.
Do not bother
to try and stop
the bleeding.
Love with the gentleness
and ferocity
of your whole
soft
tender being.
Feed the spirits
with your beauty

......

and sweetness
and ask them to show you
the way home.

STILLNESS

Let me be an apprentice to stillness.
Let me be an open vessel
filling with the vastness of each moment
overflowing with every
loving
grieving
lustful
painful
ecstatic
aching
raw
sensation.
Moments that
birth and die
contract and expand
arise and dissolve.
Let me embody exquisite gentleness
and the strength to soften
with my tendrils stretched wide
shimmering in receptivity.
Let me breathe into each question
without ever needing to know the answer.

LETTING THE GOOD GIRL DIE

I have spent much of my life being the good girl—a feminine archetype born from a place of grasping for survival in this world. We all know her well. She is nice, sweet, accommodating, agreeable, she aims to please, and is very comfortable playing small. She is never quite ready, never sure enough, never good enough, and barely audible above a whisper. She is afraid to be seen and heard, remaining in a constant state of contraction. Her truths and desires are buried deep inside, never free to breathe or be born into the world. She is detached from her sensuality, her sexuality, from the terrains of her own body. Her aspirations do not stray from that of her partner, her family, or her predestined societal roles. She feels no shortage of guilt or shame for wanting more—more expression, more passion, more freedom, just MORE.

The good girl serves us for a time. She gives us a sense of safety as we carefully navigate the world, seeking love and refuge. It means putting others' needs first, always saying yes (even when you want to say no), always wearing a cheery smiling face, and apologizing whether or not you've done anything wrong. It also means smothering the fire in your heart and between your legs, so as not to make anyone uncomfortable, or invite unwanted attention or advances. It feels like the path of least resistance to approval and acceptance... and in some ways, it is. The problem is that over time, we deaden inside... we become numb to ourselves and to the outside world. We can't make decisions, because we don't even know what it is that we truly want... we don't know who we are. We have no agency, no sovereignty, no pulse.

As I have walked through life living up to what is asked of the good girl, and eventually the good woman, the Goddess of Rage has been dancing around a volcano inside me, summoning the steam and molten lava to rise. I am angry. So often I have spoken pleasantries when there are flame-tipped arrows set in the bow of my tongue. I have compromised when I wanted to fight, tooth and nail. I have listened to those in power try to control my body, my choices, my needs, my safety, and my voice. I have covered up my body when I wanted to let my bare skin touch the breeze. I have felt myself throw up heavy armor under a man's gaze and count all the ways I feel unsafe. I want to know myself—all of my many flavors, my worth, my gifts. To dance in both my light and my shadow. To own my truth, my yes and my no.

There reaches a point when it is time for the good girl to die, and make room for the fully embodied woman. She is the wild woman, the one who carries the stories and the old ways, the one who remembers her power. There is no room for them both to live inside you if you want to thrive. This woman, like a mother wolf and her fatally injured pup, knows that the most loving gift and most fierce compassion that she can give to this wounded girl is to bring her a swift death. From this death we can rise up and can be witnessed in our beauty, our rage, our softness, our strength, our sensitivity, our sex, and our wholeness.

Instead of nice, let us be kind. Kind is not the same as nice—niceness is a passive default setting projected onto us, while kindness is an active choice that we make and embody. A kind woman is nurturing—not because it is expected of her, but because she has chosen to give her love freely. Kindness is not passivity—it is kind to speak your truth (even though others may not want to hear it), to set and maintain steady boundaries, and to hold yourself and others accountable for their actions. It is full presence and a willingness to listen. Kindness is fierce and unapologetic compassion, where your sweetness and softness meets your uncompromising strength.

As women, we hold a deep wisdom in our body and feminine essence. You do not need to look to anyone else to tell you what you already know in your blood and bones. In your womb lies a multiverse of creation, an oracle in your pussy, ancient medicine in your hands, prayers of devotion on your tongue, a fire in your belly, and an endless well of love in your heart. Your intuition will scream from every cell in your body when it needs to be heard, and we only need to listen. Trust and fully feel your emotions; allow yourself to be vulnerable and present with what is. Let yourself FEEL. Your anger is valid—let it light the ignition of transformation. Let grief wash over you and bring you to your knees. Follow joy, and let pleasure flow through your veins. There is no need to be ashamed of anything that arises, knowing that each feeling carries a message that has a place at the table.

We can become more intimate with our desires. Desire is a holy compass, illuminating the path we are meant to want to walk in the world. They point to what we yearn and long for, to what we want to create from the deep wells of our vessel. They light the way for us to walk through this world alive and awake, taking aligned actions to birth each desire into a living and breathing creation. You are allowed to be fully devoted to the altar of your own heart, to your truth, to the path that you walk. You have full permission—you ARE the permission—to take up space, to be 'too much,' to want and need and feel, and to express and give and love.

May we embrace our sensuality and sexuality. This is your life-force, your creative flame, your divine power, your sacred wildness. The natural state of the feminine is turned ON, and we have an insatiable appetite to be ravaged by the holy fire that burns inside of us. We can hold boundaries around our hearts, our bodies, and our energy field so that we feel safe to express ourselves fully from these depths, and to feel safe to fully surrender to the masculine. Do not let yourself contract under this pull, but rather, expand and unfurl—opening to the pulsing aliveness that warms your soft body, electrifies your soul, and undams your rivers.

The world is starving for embodied women. Playing nice is not serving anyone—not women, not men, not the planet at large. Lean into that place inside of you that is begging you to remember—surrender to it and unleash the holy wildfire that has been burning you alive, and penetrate the world with your truth as you rise up from the ashes.

MAGIC WOMAN

Sisters, you have diamonds
between your teeth
and spices underneath your tongue.
You make love to the air you breathe
when you exhale your truth
through red lips
smeared with honey.
Your blood runs in shades
of purple velvet and saffron sunsets.
You are both a thunderstorm
and clear blue skies
an unpredictable force
with the promise of redemption.
Do not be so quick to reveal the passcodes
to the ecstasy written between your thighs
lest you forget
the way you leave them thirsty
to drink from your river.
You were not made to be diluted.
You are a cosmic martini
made of deep oceans and fertile earth
desert winds and molten lava
with stars in your eyes
and the moon in your womb
ebbing and flowing the tides of your love
pulling us softly to your vast shores.

CHASING THE MUSE

Creativity can be a fickle and elusive lover.
The passion ebbs and flows like the tides
it cycles like the moon
it can go into deep hibernation in the shadows.

She does not want to be pursued or chased;
she is not prey to a stalking predator.
She does not fall for cheap tricks or empty promises.
She will not be pushed to act before she is ready.
She does not make negotiations for her presence.

She wants to be wooed, romanced, seduced,
and teased out from hiding.
She requires deep heart-listening
so you can hear her soft coos and whispers.

The fire must be kept burning.
She is hungry.

Feed her with the desires that are born in the soul place.
Feed her with your sweat and tears
the movement of your body
the expression of your voice.

Feed her with beauty and joy.
With sunsets, moonlight, laughter
the touch of skin
and ocean waves.

Let her see how badly you want to submit to her power
and be swept up into her holy rapture.

The muse comes when she is ready
unrestricted
so she can unleash upon you
with her seductive tendrils
to conduct a symphony of expression
through your sacred vessel
and you are left with no other choice
than to let her
take
every
last
piece of you.

OPENING TO LOVE

There are so many ways that we hold back love. It is a treasure stowed safely in our hearts, for fear that letting it flow freely in its fullest expression means imminent suffering. It may end, it may not be returned, it may make us look foolish and naive. We keep it locked up and disperse it in small and safe doses, carefully calculating the risk and reward of every morsel that is parceled out.

But let's face it—we are dying to love and be loved. When we are standing in its warm radiance, we feel connected, whole, and witnessed just as we are. It calls us into sharp presence and invites us to dance with our vulnerability. It is the ultimate teacher, the ultimate healer, the balm that eases the deepest aches. It is no wonder there is so much fear connected to the possibility of its loss—there is no greater pain than that of the loss of love, and this fear leaves us either clinging tightly and possessively to the love we have, or we avoid opening to it altogether.

Every relationship you have in this life will end. Every single one. Every family tie, every friendship, every lover, every twin flame and soul mate. Our spirits inhabit these animal bodies for a fleeting moment in time. Everything is constantly changing, evolving, dying, birthing. Who knows how long any of us have? There is no time to save up all your love for The One—the one who will stay forever, the one who will always love you back, the one who will never hurt you. Run your fingers across the battle wounds on your tender heart and feel the ley lines of your resilience. There is room for your heart to love, and break, and love again. There is room for it to be loved in return again and again. It can hold a greater capacity than you give it credit for. You are strong enough to be soft.

Loving deeply means grieving deeply. The depth of our love mirrors the depth of our grief, and while suffering may be a choice, pain is inevitable. Can you open up to love anyway? Can you hold your boundaries strong enough for you to give it fully, passionately, and unapologetically, whether or not anyone is willing to receive it? Can you love yourself harder than you've ever loved anyone or anything before? Can you stop playing it safe and let love ravage you in all its beauty and chaos? Can you embody love in the face of this crazy world? Let it be your most precious gift and sacred offering. This world is starving for your love. Give it fiercely, fully, fearlessly, give it now.

FOR THE MEN

Brothers, you have the mighty oak
in your spine
and the morning sun
in your chest.
Sing to me
with a lion underneath your tongue;
give me your soft purr
and your thundering roar.
You go down like a smooth whiskey
warming my body
with a deep
slow burn.
I'll put my pot on your stove
and let you bring me down
to a slow simmer
so I know just how you like it
to taste.
Bring your serpentine power
and your gentle touch
your sharp edges
and soft curves.
I want to wade into the depths of your waters;
let loose your tidal waves
and let me learn
to sink or swim.
Do not try
to tame
tone down
close

......

or restrain.
Bring it all to me
and let me lay my heart down
in reverence
at your feet.

AN INVITATION

I want to give all of myself to you.
I no longer wish to hold back and
tame
hush
restrain
or be afraid of being
too much
too open
or too wild
to make either one of us
feel more comfortable.
I will undress from all my armor
stripped down
to my soft, tender vulnerability.
I will claw through flesh and bone
to give my heart space to be fully exposed.
I will lay down all of my weapons
and fall to my knees
in the deepest surrender.
Let me worship you at your feet
and let me feel your reverence for me.
Put your fingers on the pulse of my desire;
feel it throbbing, aching, yearning.
Watch as I lift up my skirt
and show you all of the things
you never knew you were thirsty for.
Take a long, slow drink.
My body speaks its own language.
Come closer, let it whisper to you.

......

Listen with all of your senses.
Honey will drip from my tongue
as I sing the sweet songs of my desires in your ear.
My submission and my dominance
dance together
in my sovereignty and surrender
in my giving and receiving.
I will let my body be your playground.
Come inside
take me into your hands and mouth
and fantasies.
Let me explore all of you.
Let me touch, taste, feel, and dissolve
into your sacred terrains.
I want to be baptized in the primal fluids
of sweat and tears and all that drips
from our freshly squeezed fruits.
Slide yourself into my universe
and let go into every
touch
lick
bite
moan
scratch
kiss
thrust.
You will taste me on your tongue
long after I'm gone.
The nectar dripping down my thighs
has never tasted so sweet.

ON BURLESQUE & SEXUAL EXPRESSION

It's been two weeks since my first burlesque show with a powerhouse group of amazing humans, who I am so deeply grateful for. I am still simmering in the surprising amount of ways it has both uplifted and empowered me, and also poked and triggered me, shining a big glitter-infused spotlight into my shadows. With any big experience, I feel myself expand and stretch outward, and then contract and reflect inward. I am aware that people in my world have noticed a bit of an uptick in my sexual expression these days, and that has been met with a mix of support, confusion, and judgement. I admit that my inner angry feminist of much of my 20s would probably be shocked and dismayed, but I have long since outgrown her.

As a young woman, my sexual expression was never my own. The revealing clothing, the swing in my hips, the way I danced in clubs, even the act of sex itself was very much curated for the pleasure of a man's eyes (and his cock). I fit a lot of society's ever-changing socially acceptable beauty standards, and that brought a certain kind of attention from men that made me feel a false sense of self-worth, as well as feeling very unsafe in the world, with the careful calculations required to be sexy and yet not 'ask for it.' I accepted a lot of very bad behavior and abuse without a sense of personal sovereignty or boundaries.

It also fed into some very strange existing and unhealthy dynamics with other women. There are deeply engrained

......

reflexes for women to meet a compliment with contraction and self-deprecation. 'Oh, you think I have nice legs? Well I hate my ass. Yours is so much nicer.' Then we sit and count all the ways the other is superior. There is also a deep river of envy and competition that flows though the collective sisterhood, that has long conditioned us to compete for male attention, for success, and for worthiness, as if there are only a few measly scraps for us all to fight over.

Burlesque is essentially a sacred theater. The performers are uplifting, supporting, and celebrating each other's sexual and sensual expression with no shame. The audience can enjoy their entertainment, arousal, and sexual desires with no shame. It is a container where it is all fun, sexy, and safe. It still, however, poked at many of my wounds and conditioning. I was nervous to share what I was doing, and dragged my feet on inviting people until we were nearly sold out. I felt the reflexes to compare my face and body to what our youth and perfection obsessed society tells me is beautiful and wanted to cover myself up. I felt the reflexes to contract when another woman complimented me, and the reflexes to feel like I was less-than when another woman shined. I felt the reflexes to label what I was doing as inappropriate, narcissistic, and asking for the wrong attention, and to feel unsafe under the male gaze.

And yet, it felt incredibly electrifying to be standing fully in my body, in my sexual expression, in my feminine power, in my pleasure, side by side with the rest of the troupe, reclaiming every drop of myself I ever gave away and feeling the response that rippled out from that. We were passing out permission slips for everyone witnessing us to step into the same place of power, whether it be to give or receive this kind of expression. There are old and new beliefs and ways of being that are still wrestling a bit inside me, and there has been years (that echo decades and even centuries) of accumulated conditioning around gender roles and sexual shaming and suppression—it's going to take some time to unravel. I am feeling a lightness and freedom in letting it all go.

I would like to say that I don't care what people think of me, but I do. I still feel the weight of expectations and judgement. But my need to express myself as one whole, multifaceted woman has been outweighing that burden more and more. I realize that a burlesque performance, a photo of my bare skin, or even a poem infused with sex could all be viewed in shameful ways, and it may push people away. But each time I dip my toes further into these waters, I shed another layer of shame, another layer of conditioning, another mask, and feel more at home in my skin.

My sexuality, my sensuality, my desires and my pleasure are my own. I want other women to meet me in that place— celebrating and uplifting each other in every way. We are not fighting over scraps, we are tapping into infinite possibility and desire, reclaiming and remembering our immense feminine power. I want men to meet me in that place— standing fully in their personal and sexual sovereignty, expressing their deepest desires, and reclaiming and remembering their immense masculine power. Imagine the alchemy that can be birthed from there?

SUNDAY MORNING

I want your Sunday morning
quivering breath
with the dew glistening on your skin
after you have just had me
for breakfast.

FIRE AND WATER

My darling woman
you do not need to choose
and you do not need permission.
You are both fire and water
with feet planted in the earth
and ancestors at your back.
You can be kind and gentle
and still have your sharp tongue.
You can be both soft and strong
with your heart open wide
and backbone tall.
Turn your face up towards the warmth
of your own light
and sink down
into your fertile darkness.
There may be flowers in your hair
but there is a holy fire between your hips.
You can be a woman
who likes to make love
and whisper softly
and a woman
who likes to fuck
and scream loudly.
Put your pot on the stove and let
your love
your rage
your sweetness
your bitter sting
your softness

your rough edges
your resistance
your surrender
all simmer down
bubble up
and boil over
into one big
glorious
and beautiful mess
and watch the magnetic pull
of moth
to your wild flame.

OF EARTH AND SKY

My spirit lives in a house made of earth and sky
There are butterflies in my eyelashes
Stars in my eyes
Rose petals line my lips
I dress my body with moonlight
My spine is stacked with the bones of my ancestors
A warm breeze carries prayers from my mouth to the divine
A thousand petaled lotus blooms eternally in my chest
My tears are a soft summer rain
When I speak, honey drips from my tongue and my voice
sounds like thunder
There is fire in my belly
My hips and breasts hold the peaks of ancient mountains
The ocean ebbs and flows in my veins
My feet are roots that dig deep into fertile ground
I hold the universe in my womb
A volcano sits between my legs that erupts with milk, and
nectar, and blood, and fire
I give birth to myself,
again and again,
until one day
I am swallowed
by the earthly body
that I came from

DEVOTION

You can go to all the workshops and retreats
and read all of the books
and do all of the practices
and go to the holy places
and sing the songs of worship
and push your mind and body to the edge
and work with all the gurus and teachers
and do all the right things

and yet...

It's the flutter of a butterfly
a soft kiss from a lover's lips
the sweetness of fresh berries
the release of tears
a piece of art
the buzzing of a honeybee
a spontaneous dance
the scent of a rose
a breeze against your cheek
bare feet on the earth
the pluck of a guitar string
a burning sunset
a full-bellied laugh
the booming of thunder
that breaks your heart open
and brings you

down
to
your
knees

It is speaking, listening, seeing, feeling, moving, acting from
the heart
that pulls the sweetest prayer
from your lips
that your tongue
has ever tasted

VOWS

To you, Gina:

To your sweet inner child, I vow to honor you. You are held, loved, and protected. You are free to play, express, be joyful and be silly. You are worthy of all the love that surrounds you, all the love you desire, and all the love that is given to you. You are safe, you are heard, you are not alone. I love you.

To the mother in you, I vow to honor you. You hold all the cosmic power of creation in your womb, and you birth beauty and love into the world with the way you nurture, the way you love, the art you create, the words you weave, and through the incredible light of your being. I love you.

To your pussy, I vow to honor you. I will prioritize your pleasure and desire, and trust you as my oracle, because I know my intuition lives inside of you. I honor your cycles and seasons, and love you through all of them. You are the gateway to ecstasy, and I will only allow those worthy of your power to enter the threshold. I love you.

To the lover, partner and wife in you, I vow to honor you. You are worthy of your heart's deepest longing and desire. You are easy to love, and it is a gift to be loved by you. There is no limit to the love and devotion and worship that is possible for you to receive and surrender to. It is safe for you to be loved fully, and for you to express all the love and devotion in your heart. I love you.

......

To your whole, beautiful being, I vow to honor you. To your inner man, your inner woman, to everything in between, and the union of all parts of you as one. I love you.

I vow to be patient and kind to you, and love you with a gentle fierceness that reminds you to always chose yourself.

I vow to continue to work to unravel and release stories, patterns, and wounds that hold you back in any way, and support you as you continue to unfurl into the fullest, happiest, healthiest expression of your being.

I vow to open to all of the abundance that is waiting for you, because you are worthy of it all, and have the capacity to hold it.

I vow to honor and trust the divine timing of your life, your unfolding, and your evolution. It's never too late, and your love was never wasted. You are right on time.

I vow to love you through heartache and disappointment, through the deepest grief, and love you in your joy and pleasure.

I vow to allow you to take up space beyond the reaches of what you thought was possible, and celebrate you each time you stretch out a little further. It is safe to express the fullness of who you are, and the expression of your wholeness is a gift to the world. I vow to love you, all of you, always.

GRATITUDE

Thank you to the people who encouraged me, supported me, pushed me, held me, helped me do all the hard things, and acted as doulas through this creative birthing process.

Thank you to my family, friends, kindred spirits, and lovers for uplifting me, witnessing me, loving me so deeply, and allowing me the gift of loving you in return.

Thank you to my teachers—those who name themselves as such, and those who have taught me through simply being who they are. To the teachers that show up as failures, heartbreak, pain, grief, and love.

Thank you to the Goddess, God, and Great Spirit. To Mother Earth, Father Sky, Brother Sun and Sister Moon. To Star Cousins, Ancestors, Guardians and Guides. To the Waters. To the Elements and the Four Directions. To all my kin of Land, Sea and Sky.

Thank you to the misfits, the wild ones, the poets, the tricksters, the artists, the movers and shakers, the deep thinkers, the silly and playful, the lovers, the grievers, the children, the elders, the witches, the healers, the ones who show us what it means to be alive.

ABOUT ME

I am a student of magic, love, grief, intimacy, myth and story, ritual arts, and the wild and vast terrain that we call nature.

My writing is inspired by the exploration of good questions, by relating with my human and non-human kin, and by my pursuit of beauty and awe.

I hope to live with my heart open, my voice free, my mind curious, and my feet rooted in love.

www.ginapuorro.com

Made in United States
North Haven, CT
21 January 2023

31384912R00096